TESTIMONIAL

This is a handbook for those who are eager to become sales masters, but are asking themselves, "What do I do next?" "How do I deal with a procrastinating client?" or "How can I effectively present my product?" Hopkins conveys instructions and suggestions through a variety of sales conversations.

- Rolf Dobelli

....

I wouldn't have made the decision to get into sales without this book. Everything you need from prospecting, presenting, closing, to developing the right attitude are in this book. Tom Hopkins is a winner and a giant in the field of selling. Even veterans will get something of value from this book.

- Trent Rollow

....

I first read this book when I was in the executive search business and it was instrumental in increasing my effectiveness at selling and developing clients. Tom Hopkins' techniques and suggestions are timeless and well worth the read.

- J. W. Ward

....

Tom takes the "how to" approach to the sales process. He helps us from the very beginning of the sales process all the way to getting referrals. He helps us to rid ourselves of using words and strategies that can easily kill a sale.

- Rollis Fontenot

....

If you cannot sell, you cannot succeed... Rarely have I come across a book so passionately written about the subject. Not only does Tom highly succeed in explaining the art of selling, but he also outlines the very important aspects of psychology (notably fear of failure). He covers beautifully the basics of time management (in line with 80/20 or Steven Covey). Champions are made, not born!

- Franco Arda

HOW TO Master the *Art* of SELLING

from
SmarterComics

by **Tom Hopkins**

Illustrated by Bob Byrne

Adapted by Cullen Bunn

Executive Editor
Corey Michael Blake

Creative Director
Nathan Brown

rtc
A Round Table Companies Production
www.roundtablepress.com

INTRODUCTION

My sales career began in the field of real estate sales. I was 19 years young, trying to make it in a mature man's industry. Not only did I live in a rented apartment but my only means of transportation was a motorcycle. To make matters worse, I didn't own a suit. With all those strikes against me, I knew I would have to work harder than others. I would have to work longer than others. But, my belief in the business and the opportunity for success it offered me carried me forward. My enthusiasm for helping people live the American dream of owning a home closed as many sales for me as my skills.

Speaking of skills, initially they were quite dismal. My first six months in the business I only made one sale. Then, I learned of a sales skill seminar coming to my area. I hadn't known there was such a thing but knew I had to learn more if I was going to succeed. That program not only turned my life around, it opened my mind to a whole world of education I previously did not know existed. Becoming a dedicated student, my skills continued to improve and my income continued to grow. I made selling my hobby. I watched and analyzed every selling situation I could see around me and constantly applied new ideas to my presentations. I'll admit there was some trial and error (the error part anyway) but I learned from those experiences, as well.

The "happily-ever-after" ending is that I achieved my goal of becoming a millionaire a few years ahead of schedule. My success in that area eventually led me into training and writing this book.

Because I achieved great results in real estate sales, I was often asked to speak about my strategies and tactics. Hating public speaking with a passion, I often refused. But my mentor at the time, the late J. Douglas Edwards, told me that if "you do what you fear most, you will control that fear." So, I became a student of public speaking. I wasn't very good at it but the audiences loved the how-to's I was sharing with them. Eventually, my speaking skills improved and I changed careers—becoming a full-time trainer.

After people from other industries besides real estate started having success with what I was teaching, I realized we needed to provide it in different formats. Audio recordings were made. Video training programs were created. And How to Master the Art of Selling was written. Other books have been written as well, but this remains the core—the foundation—of all of my training.

Moving forward to today, our audios, which were once only available on cassette tapes, can be found on CDs and in MP3 formats. Our videos are on DVD and streamed on the internet. Some of our written materials are available for electronic readers and as e-books—and now, in the graphic novel format. I have to admit this rendition of my selling skills training has been the most fun to work on. Paring a nearly 400-page book down to its essential elements was a challenge. I hope you find it as beneficial and enjoyable to read as I found it to create.

Wishing you greatness in your selling endeavors,

Tom Hopkins

THE WORDS YOU SPEAK CAN DESTROY
SALES AS WELL AS CREATE THEM, SO THINK
OF YOUR MOUTH AS A SHARP-EDGED TOOL
THAT MUST BE USED WISELY.

LEARN THE RIGHT WORDS TO SAY AND HOW
TO SAY THEM AND YOU'LL BE ABLE TO
CREATE WIN-WIN SELLING SITUATIONS.

HOW TO
Master the *Art* of
SELLING

from
SmarterComics™

I LEARNED A LONG TIME AGO THAT SELLING IS THE HIGHEST-PAID HARD WORK—AND THE LOWEST-PAID EASY WORK—THERE IS..

AND I FOUND OUT ANOTHER EXCITING THING ABOUT SELLING—THE CHOICE WAS MINE, ALL MINE.

BY MYSELF, I COULD MAKE IT THE HIGHEST-PAID HARD WORK ...

... OR I COULD MAKE IT THE LOWEST-PAID EASY WORK.

THE WHOLE POINT OF THIS BOOK IS THAT THE SKILLS, KNOWLEDGE, AND DRIVE WITHIN YOU ARE WHAT WILL MAKE YOU GREAT ... AND THESE QUALITIES CAN BE **EXPANDED** AND **INTENSIFIED**— IF YOU'RE WILLING TO INVEST THE TIME, EFFORT, AND MONEY IN YOURSELF.

KNOWLEDGE

SKILLS

DRIVE

LET'S BEGIN BY TALKING ABOUT THE **ADVANTAGES OF SELLING.**

THE FIRST ADVANTAGE—AND THE REASON I LOVE SELLING—IS THE *FREEDOM OF EXPRESSION.*

SALES IS ONE OF THE FEW PROFESSIONS IN WHICH YOU CAN BE YOURSELF AND CAN, IN ESSENCE, DO WHAT YOU WANT TO DO AS LONG AS IT'S APPROPRIATE FOR YOUR PRODUCT AND CLIENTS. IN SALES, YOU COMPETE IN AN ARENA WHERE RESOURCEFULNESS AND PERSEVERANCE ARE DEMANDED AND VALUED.

THE SECOND ADVANTAGE OF SELLING IS THAT YOU HAVE THE *FREEDOM TO BECOME AS SUCCESSFUL AS YOU'D LIKE TO BE.* IN THIS PROFESSION, NO ONE LIMITS YOUR INCOME POTENTIAL BUT YOU.

THE THIRD ADVANTAGE IS THAT IT IS A *DAILY CHALLENGE.*

FOR THE SALESPERSON, EVERY DAY IS AN ADVENTURE.

THE FOURTH ADVANTAGE IS THAT SALES OFFERS HIGH POTENTIAL FOR RETURNS FROM A LOW CAPITAL INVESTMENT.

THE FIFTH ELEMENT OF SELLING IS THAT IT'S *FUN.* MY PHILOSOPHY IS THAT IF IT'S NOT FUN, IT'S NOT WORTH DOING.

THE SIXTH ADVANTAGE OF THE SELLING PROFESSION IS THAT IT'S *SATISFYING.* IT'S A THRILL TO KNOW YOU'VE HELPED SOMEONE MAKE THE DECISION TO OWN YOUR PRODUCT.

I'VE ALSO LEARNED THAT THERE IS NO SUCH THING AS A NATURAL-BORN SALES WONDER. THERE HAS *NEVER* BEEN A GREAT SALESPERSON WHO WAS *BORN GREAT.*

THIS IS A MYTH THAT CUTS TWO WAYS, AND DON'T LET IT EXCUSE YOU FROM THE HARD WORK OF LEARNING HOW TO BE COMPETENT IN YOUR SALES CAREER. WHETHER YOU THINK YOU ARE A WONDER OR A NON-WONDER, YOU STILL HAVE TO LEARN IF YOU'RE GOING TO BE A *REAL CHAMPION.*

GREAT SALESPEOPLE, LIKE GREAT ATHLETES, SIMPLY DO THE BASICS VERY WELL.

THERE ARE *SEVEN BASICS* THAT'LL MAKE YOU AS GREAT AS YOU WANT TO BE.

PROSPECTING

THIS MAY MAKE YOU NERVOUS, BUT DON'T LET IT. IF YOU DON'T LIKE TO PROSPECT, IT'S BECAUSE NO ONE TAUGHT YOU THE PROFESSIONAL WAY TO DO IT.

MAKING ORIGINAL CONTACT THE PROFESSIONAL WAY

WE ALL MEET PEOPLE ALL THE TIME. THE KEY TO SUCCESS IN SELLING IS TO REFINE YOUR SKILLS DURING THESE INITIAL CONTACTS TO BECOME MEMORABLE TO OTHERS ... WHILE REMEMBERING AS MUCH ABOUT THEM AS POSSIBLE.

QUALIFICATION

IF YOU SPEND YOUR TIME TALKING TO THE WRONG PEOPLE, IT DOESN'T MATTER HOW ELOQUENTLY YOU PRESENT YOUR PRODUCT OR SERVICE.

PRESENTATION

YOU MUST PRESENT YOUR PRODUCT IN SUCH A WAY THAT THE POTENTIAL CLIENT SEES THAT IT'S JUST WHAT THEY HAD IN MIND ALL ALONG.

HANDLING OBJECTIONS

I DON'T KNOW ... WE PURCHASED SIMILAR SOFTWARE LAST YEAR AND NEVER USED IT.

I UNDERSTAND. IT SOUNDS LIKE HAVING SOME ASSISTANCE WITH SET UP AND TRAINING WOULD BE OF INTEREST TO YOU. AM I RIGHT?

WHEN FACED WITH OBJECTIONS, YOU HAVE TO SMILE, AND LEARN THE RIGHT APPROACH TO CLOSE THE SALE.

CLOSING THE SALE

CLOSING EFFECTIVELY IS PART ART, PART SCIENCE ... AND THOSE ELEMENTS CAN BE LEARNED.

REFERRALS

IF YOUR CLIENTS ARE HAPPY, THEY'LL WANT SOMEONE ELSE TO BE HAPPY, TOO. I'LL TEACH YOU HOW TO GET SOLID, QUALIFIED REFERRALS EVERY TIME, IF YOU'RE WILLING.

IF THE PROFESSIONAL GOLFER USES A CLUB, THE TENNIS PLAYER A RACQUET, AND THE CARPENTER A HAMMER, WHAT DO WE PROFESSIONAL SALESPEOPLE USE?

YOUR PRIMARY TOOL— *YOUR MOUTH*— MUST BE USED WITH CONFIDENCE.

THE WORDS YOU SPEAK CAN DESTROY SALES AS WELL AS CREATE THEM, SO THINK OF YOUR MOUTH AS A SHARP-EDGED TOOL THAT MUST BE USED WISELY.

LEARN THE RIGHT WORDS TO SAY AND HOW TO SAY THEM AND YOU'LL BE ABLE TO CREATE WIN-WIN SELLING SITUATIONS.

I'VE GATHERED A LIST OF *TWELVE PERSONALITY TRAITS OR CHARACTERISTICS* COMMON TO THOSE WHO ACHIEVE CHAMPION-STATUS IN SELLING.

AS WE GO THROUGH THIS LIST, THINK ABOUT HOW YOU MEASURE UP.

YOU KNOW CHAMPIONS WHEN THEY WALK THROUGH THE DOOR.

THEY REFLECT A SENSE OF UNIQUE INDIVIDUALITY AND PERSONAL COMPETENCE THAT'S FAR MORE IMPRESSIVE THAN MERE GOOD LOOKS.

CHAMPIONS TAKE TREMENDOUS PRIDE IN THE PROFESSION OF SELLING AND IN THEMSELVES AS HUMAN BEINGS.

CHAMPIONS RADIATE CONFIDENCE.

CHAMPIONS CLOSE WARMLY.

EVENTUALLY, THE VULTURES WHO THINK OF SELLING AS NOTHING MORE THAN AGGRESSION WILL BE DRIVEN OUT BY ENLIGHTENED SALESPEOPLE WHO QUALIFY THEIR PROSPECTS, CARE ABOUT THEIR CUSTOMERS, AND MAKE SURE THEIR CLIENTS DERIVE REAL BENEFITS FROM THEIR PURCHASES.

CHAMPIONS LOOK TO ONLY ONE PERSON FOR THEIR SELF-ASSURANCE, AND THAT ONE PERSON IS THEMSELVES.

CHAMPIONS WANT TO GET RICH. THAT'S RIGHT, *RICH*... BY HELPING OTHERS GET WHAT THEY WANT.

CHAMPIONS HAVE THE BURNING DESIRE TO ACHIEVE.

ONLY YOU CAN MEASURE HOW MUCH DESIRE YOU HAVE. IF YOU HAVE THE POTENTIAL TO BE A CHAMPION, YOU WILL NEVER QUIT TRYING TO ACHIEVE YOUR GOALS, NO MATTER HOW MANY CHALLENGES YOU ENCOUNTER.

CHAMPIONS LEARN WHAT THEIR FEARS ARE, THEN DO WHAT THEY FEAR MOST AND OVERCOME IT.

CHAMPIONS KNOW THAT, NO MATTER HOW GOOD THEY GET, THEY ARE STILL GOING TO FAIL SOME OF THE TIME BETWEEN THEIR SUCCESSES. IT'S ALL PART OF THE GAME WE CALL SELLING.

SO THEY DON'T HAVE TO HIDE THEIR TRUE FEELINGS WHILE THEY ARE FAILING BECAUSE THEY ARE STILL FILLED WITH ENTHUSIASM.

CHAMPIONS REALLY CARE ABOUT THEIR CLIENTS, AND THIS TRUE FEELING COMES THROUGH LOUD AND CLEAR TO THE PEOPLE THEY'RE HELPING TO ENJOY THE BENEFITS OF THEIR OFFERING.

CHAMPIONS DON'T TAKE REJECTION PERSONALLY.

CHAMPIONS BELIEVE IN CONTINUING EDUCATION. THEY STUDY TECHNIQUE. THEY LEARN NEW SKILLS.

HERE ARE THREE METHODS OF DEVELOPING THE BURNING DESIRE TO SUCCEED THAT CAN'T BE DENIED. THEY WORK—IF YOU WANT THEM TO.

YOU HAVE TO HAVE THE DESIRE TO SUCCEED AND MAKE THE EFFORT TO MAKE THIS TRAINING WORK.

THE GREATEST OBSTACLE TO DEVELOPING DESIRE IS OUR CONVICTION THAT WE'LL NEVER BE ABLE TO SATISFY IT, SO THE SAFEST COURSE OF ACTION IS TO DISCOURAGE THE DESIRE AND AVOID THE FRUSTRATION.

THE FACT IS, THOUGH, THAT THERE ISN'T ANY EXCUSE FOR NOT ACHIEVING SUCCESS.

FOCUS ON THE SPECIFIC THINGS YOU WANT. MAKE AGREEMENTS WITH YOURSELF. DON'T MAKE YOURSELF WORK FOR NOTHING.

IF I DO THIS ....

I GET THAT

START WITH A REALISTIC INCREASE. SOMETHING YOU TRULY BELIEVE YOU CAN ACHIEVE.

TAKE IT IN STEPS.

IF YOU'VE NEVER MADE MORE THAN MINIMUM WAGE, DON'T AIM FOR HALF A MILLION IN THE FIRST YEAR.

FOR A CHAMPION, PRACTICE MAKES PERFECT. PRACTICE THE WORDS AND RESPONSES YOU'LL BE USING IN YOUR MEETINGS AND PRESENTATIONS.

POWER CLOSE: THE ECONOMIC TRUTH

PRACTICE THE PRECISE WORDS YOU'LL USE UNTIL THEY'RE SECOND NATURE. DRILL YOURSELF ON DELIVERING THEM WITH CLARITY AND CONVICTION.

REHEARSE DELIVERING THEM IN AS LIFELIKE A SITUATION AS YOU CAN CREATE, WORKING IN COOPERATION WITH PEOPLE WHO CARE ABOUT YOUR SUCCESS IN THE BUSINESS.

QUESTIONS ARE THE MOST POWERFUL TOOLS A CHAMPION CAN USE. THERE ARE MANY TYPES OF QUESTIONS, BUT HERE ARE THREE PRINCIPLES FOR QUESTION-ASKING POWER.

FIRST, ALWAYS ESTABLISH A BOND BEFORE GETTING DOWN TO BUSINESS.

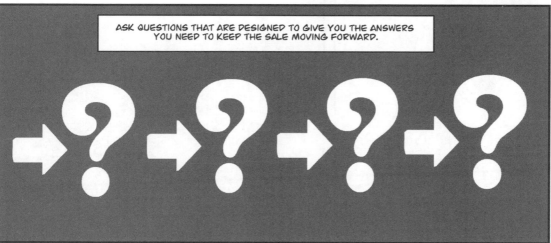

ASK QUESTIONS THAT ARE DESIGNED TO GIVE YOU THE ANSWERS YOU NEED TO KEEP THE SALE MOVING FORWARD.

ASK DISCOVERY QUESTIONS THAT WILL REVEAL THE PRODUCTS AND SERVICES THEY WANT TO OWN.

AND WHAT IS THE BIGGEST CHALLENGE YOUR ORGANIZATION IS FACING CURRENTLY?

REMEMBER THAT YOU CAN'T LEAD PEOPLE TO DECISIONS UNTIL YOU MAKE THE DECISIONS.

COMPETITION ANALYSIS

YOUR JOB IS TO HELP YOUR CLIENTS MAKE DECISIONS THAT ARE TRULY GOOD FOR THEM. IF YOU CAN'T HELP THEM MAKE BETTER DECISIONS, WHAT DO THEY NEED YOU FOR?

NOW, LET'S TALK ABOUT CREATING THE **SELLING CLIMATE**...

REMEMBER THAT CHAMPIONS ONLY SELL THE FEATURES AND BENEFITS THAT THE PROSPECT WANTS TO BUY.

DON'T SELL WHAT YOU WANT. SELL WHAT THEY WANT.

CHAMPIONS DON'T SELL BENEFITS BEFORE FINDING OUT WHAT BENEFITS THE PROSPECT WANTS AND NEEDS.

CHAMPIONS ALSO SELL TO THE PEOPLE WHO CAN BUY.

MANY SALESPEOPLE SPEND HOURS WITH PEOPLE WHO CAN'T SAY 'YES.'

IN MANY CASES, YOU'LL BE TOLD THAT NO ONE INDIVIDUAL MAKES THE DECISION YOU SEEK.

ALL BUYING DECISIONS ARE MADE BY COMMITTEE.

THERE ARE FEW SITUATIONS IN SALES MORE COMPLEX AND EASY TO BOTCH THAN THE UNREACHABLE COMMITTEE. FLEXIBILITY IN THESE SITUATIONS—AND SOME SKILL IN HANDLING GNOMES—IS IMPORTANT.

BEWARE:

THE GNOMES IN THE BACK ROOM ARE INSECURE, AND THEY CAN BE JEALOUS OF THE POWER WIELDED BY A DECISION-MAKER OR COMMITTEE.

YOU NEED TO MAKE THE GNOMES FEEL IMPORTANT AND POWERFUL IN ORDER TO GAIN THEIR TRUST AND GET THEM TO HELP YOU.

HAVE FAITH IN THE VALUE AND IMPORTANCE OF YOUR OFFERING.

MAKE SURE YOU'RE WORKING WITH THE RIGHT GNOME, NOT SOME CHAIR WARMER WHOSE MAIN JOB IS GETTING RID OF SALESPEOPLE.

THERE ARE TWO KINDS OF GNOMES: THOSE WHO RELISH DISPLAYING THEIR POWER BY COMMITTING THEMSELVES, AND THOSE WHO'LL NEVER COMMIT THEMSELVES.

NEVER TRY TO GET AN IRONCLAD COMMITMENT FROM A RELUCTANT GNOME. IT CAN'T BE DONE.

IF YOU CAN'T SELL A GNOME WITHIN A REASONABLE TIME, AND IF THE ORGANIZATION IS WORTH MORE OF YOUR TIME, TRY AN END RUN.

YOU RISK MAKING AN ENEMY OF THE GNOME, BUT WHAT DO YOU HAVE TO LOSE? YOU'VE ALREADY LOST-OR FAILED TO GAIN-THE GNOME'S SUPPORT.

MANY OF US TRY TO SELL OUR PRODUCTS THROUGH LOGIC.

BUT SELDOM DO PEOPLE BUY LOGICALLY. PEOPLE BUY *EMOTIONALLY*, THEN DEFEND THEIR DECISIONS WITH LOGIC.

POSITIVE EMOTIONS TRIGGER SALES. NEGATIVE EMOTIONS DESTROY SALES.

AS YOU DEVELOP THE SKILL TO EVOKE EMOTIONS IN YOUR CLIENTS, ALWAYS REMEMBER—YOU CAN DESTROY A SALE AS RAPIDLY AS YOU CAN CREATE ONE THROUGH THE CLUMSY USE OF, OR LACK OF CONTROL OVER, THE EMOTIONAL SETTING.

THE TRUTH IS ... ONE NEGATIVE CAN WIPE OUT MANY POSITIVES.

YOU MUST USE SENSES THAT SELL THE EMOTIONS.

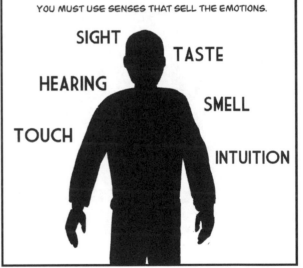

SIGHT

TASTE

HEARING

SMELL

TOUCH

INTUITION

CHAMPIONS DO THEIR BEST TO GET AS MANY SENSES INVOLVED AS POSSIBLE. THE MORE SENSES YOU INVOLVE, THE BETTER YOUR ODDS OF MAKING A SALE.

IF YOU'RE THE KIND OF PERSON WHO'S ALL TALK, TALK, TALK, TALK, TALK, HOW MANY SENSES ARE YOU INVOLVING?

EVERYONE GETS DOWN EVERY NOW AND AGAIN. WE ALL HAVE TIMES WHEN WE JUST CAN'T GET UP AND DO WHAT WE NEED TO DO.

BUT YOU'LL QUICKLY LEARN THAT YOU SIMPLY WON'T MAKE AS MUCH MONEY WHEN YOU'RE DEPRESSED AS YOU DO WHEN YOU'RE ENTHUSIASTIC.

IF YOU'RE DEPRESSED NOW ABOUT YOUR SALES PERFORMANCE ... EVER HAVE BEEN IN THE PAST ... OR THINK IT'S A POSSIBILITY THAT YOU COULD BE IN THE FUTURE, YOU NEED TO LOOK TOWARDS YOUR *SOURCES OF MOTIVATION*.

WEEPEX

THE FIRST MOTIVATOR OF THE GREAT SALESPERSON IS *MONEY*.

MONEY ALLOWS YOU TO GET THE THINGS YOU WANT AND NEED. MONEY IS GOOD SO LONG AS WHAT YOU EARN IS IN DIRECT PROPORTION TO THE SERVICE YOU GIVE.

THE SECOND MOTIVATOR IS *SECURITY*.

THE THIRD MOTIVATOR IS *ACHIEVEMENT*.

THE FOURTH MOTIVATOR IS **RECOGNITION**.

ACCEPTANCE BY OTHERS IS THE FIFTH MOTIVATOR.

THE SIXTH MOTIVATOR IS **SELF-ACCEPTANCE**.

SELF-ACCEPTANCE IS THE STATE OF BEING YOUR OWN PERSON. SELF-ACCEPTANCE MARKS THE DAY WHEN THE OPINIONS OF OTHERS DON'T MATTER ANYMORE.

FAMILY IS THE SEVENTH MOTIVATOR.

YOU CAN WORK HARD TO ACHIEVE, EARN MONEY, BE RECOGNIZED, ATTAIN SECURITY, HAVE OTHERS ACCEPT YOU AND ACCEPT YOURSELF.

BUT IF YOU DON'T GIVE YOUR LOVED ONES A HIGH LEVEL OF "SERVICE"—BEING INVOLVED IN THEIR LIVES, PROVIDING THEM WITH RECOGNITION AND SECURITY, AND SO ON—YOU MAY FIND YOURSELF ALONE.

NOW WE'RE GOING TO TALK ABOUT WHY PEOPLE DON'T GET THE THINGS THEY'RE MOTIVATED TO SEEK—THE DEMOTIVATORS.

THE FIRST DEMOTIVATOR IS THE **FEAR OF LOSING SECURITY.**

IF YOU REFUSE TO GIVE UP ANYTHING THAT YOU HAVE NOW, WHERE WILL THE SPACE, TIME, MONEY, AND ENERGY COME FROM FOR NEW ACHIEVEMENTS?

FEAR OF FAILURE IS THE SECOND DEMOTIVATOR.

BUT THE ONLY WAY TO AVOID FAILURE IS TO JUST NEVER TRY.

REMEMBER, IF YOU DO WHAT YOU FEAR MOST, YOU CONTROL FEAR. IF YOU DON'T CONTROL FEAR, FEAR CONTROLS YOU.

THE THIRD DEMOTIVATOR IS **SELF-DOUBT.**

COMMIT YOURSELF TO SUCCESS IN SALES. DON'T BRAG ABOUT ALL YOU'RE GOING TO DO, BUT DON'T EXCUSE YOURSELF FROM ALL-OUT EFFORT, EITHER.

DON'T PREDICT YOUR OWN FAILURE AND THEN SET OUT TO PROVE HOW GOOD YOU ARE AT MAKING PREDICTIONS.

THE FOURTH DEMOTIVATOR IS THE *PAIN OF CHANGE.*

BUT DON'T FIGHT CHANGE. MAKE IT WORK FOR YOU.

THAT'S EASIER SAID THAN DONE, BUT HERE'S HOW TO MAKE CHANGE A POSITIVE FORCE FOR YOU.

FACE THE ISSUE SQUARELY BY THINKING THROUGH YOUR EMOTIONAL FEAR OF CHANGE.

KEEP THE BEST OF THE OLD IN YOUR LIFE SO THAT YOU'LL HAVE A STRONG EMOTIONAL FOUNDATION ON WHICH TO BUILD HELPFUL CHANGE.

EVERY DAY, TELL SOMEONE THAT YOU'RE QUICK TO ADOPT NEW IDEAS, THAT YOU LIKE SAMPLING NEW THINGS, THAT YOU'RE ALWAYS LEARNING, CHANGING, AND GROWING. KEEP SAYING THAT AND YOU'LL BELIEVE IT, ACT ON IT, AND MAKE IT TRUE.

THE PAIN OF CHANGE IS ALWAYS FORGOTTEN WHEN THE BENEFITS OF THAT CHANGE ARE REALIZED.

NOBODY LIKES REJECTION, BUT REJECTION COMES WITH THE TERRITORY IN SELLING.

THERE ARE FIVE ATTITUDES TOWARDS FAILURE THAT CAN HELP YOU MAXIMIZE YOUR ABILITY TO DEAL WITH REJECTION AND REJECT FAILURE.

REJECTION AS A *LEARNING EXPERIENCE*.

REJECTION CAN BE A LESSON IN PRACTICAL SALESMANSHIP THAT IS VERY SPECIFIC TO WHEN, WHERE, WHAT AND HOW YOU SELL.

REJECTION AS *COURSE CORRECTION*.

IF YOU'RE OFF COURSE, IT TAKES NEGATIVE FEEDBACK TO GET YOU BACK ON COURSE.

THE *HUMOR* IN REJECTION.

DO EVERYTHING POSSIBLE TO HOLD A SALE TOGETHER. BUT IF IT FRACTURES ANYWAY, THEN LOOK AT THE LIGHTER SIDE.

REJECTION AS **PRACTICE**.

REJECTION MEANS THAT YOU'VE HAD THE OPPORTUNITY TO PRACTICE YOUR TECHNIQUES AND PERFECT YOUR PERFORMANCE.

REJECTION AS **PART OF THE GAME**.

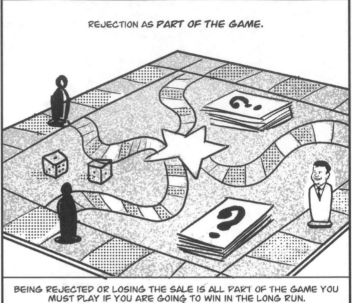

BEING REJECTED OR LOSING THE SALE IS ALL PART OF THE GAME YOU MUST PLAY IF YOU ARE GOING TO WIN IN THE LONG RUN.

HERE IS MY BASIC PHILOSOPHY—MY **CREED OF CHAMPIONS**. . .

I AM NOT JUDGED BY THE NUMBER OF TIMES I FAIL, BUT BY THE NUMBER OF TIMES I SUCCEED, AND THE NUMBER OF TIMES I SUCCEED IS IN DIRECT PROPORTION TO THE NUMBER OF TIMES I CAN FAIL AND KEEP TRYING.

OF COURSE, AN ESSENTIAL PART OF SALES IS FINDING SOMEONE TO SELL TO. THIS IS CALLED PROSPECTING!

THERE'S A SIMPLE SECRET TO HELP YOU SUCCEED IN PROSPECTING, AND IT CAN BE SUMMED UP BY THIS DRAWING.

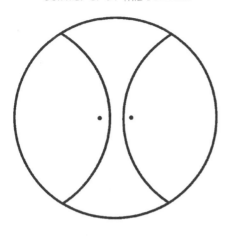

WHAT'S IT MEAN? SIMPLE.

IF YOU MEET 20 PEOPLE BELLY TO BELLY (OR FACE TO FACE IF YOU PREFER) EVERY DAY, YOU CAN'T HELP BUT SUCCEED.

PREPARE A LIST OF EVERYONE YOU KNOW IN THE CONTACT MANAGEMENT PROGRAM IN YOUR COMPUTER.

START WITH MOM AND DAD, BROTHERS AND SISTERS, AUNTS AND UNCLES. DON'T FORGET GRANDMA AND GRANDPA.

THEN MOVE TO YOUR BEST FRIENDS AND NEIGHBORS. USE YOUR ADDRESS LIST AND THE CONTACTS IN YOUR PHONE LIST. USE YOUR CHRISTMAS CARD LIST IF YOU HAVE ONE.

WHY DO YOU WANT GRANDMA ON YOUR BUSINESS CONTACT LIST?

BECAUSE GRANDMA KNOWS A LOT OF OTHER PEOPLE!

ONCE YOU HAVE YOUR LIST COMPLETE, DRAFT A SHORT LETTER ABOUT YOUR NEW POSITION. EXPLAIN THE BENEFITS YOUR PRODUCT OFFERS-NOT THE FEATURES, NOT THE TECHNICAL DETAILS.

DON'T TELL TOO MUCH, JUST ENOUGH SO PEOPLE GET THE GIST OF WHAT YOU'RE DOING.

END BY ASKING THEM TO KEEP YOU IN MIND WHEN THE SUBJECT OF WHATEVER YOU'RE SELLING COMES UP.

FOLLOW UP WITH PHONE CALLS TO THE TOP TEN OR TWENTY PEOPLE ON YOUR LIST WHO WOULD BE MOST LIKELY TO HELP YOU.

TO KEEP YOUR LIST-AND YOUR BUSINESS-GROWING, ADD EVERYONE YOU TALK WITH **EVERY DAY.**

NOTES:
Referral from Granny. Sending marketing materials

AFTER COMPLETING A SALE, CHAMPIONS SAY ....

I MUST FIND TWO MORE GOOD POTENTIAL FUTURE CLIENTS FOR THIS WONDERFUL OPPORTUNITY.

ONE OF THE BEST THINGS ABOUT SELLING, ESPECIALLY IN THE BEGINNING, IS THAT BEING BUSY AT FIRST LEADS TO BUSINESS. IN OTHER WORDS, **ACTIVITY BREEDS PRODUCTIVITY.**

INBOX OUTBOX

NOW, YOU HAVE TO BE ACTIVE AT THE RIGHT THINGS, SUCH AS ...

KEEPING UP WITH INDUSTRY NEWS ...

THE TIMES

MAKING PRESENTATIONS ...

SENDING THANK YOU NOTES, MAILINGS, BROCHURES, E-MAILS, NEWSLETTERS— WHATEVER— TO GENERATE LEADS FOR YOURSELF RATHER THAN WAITING FOR COMPANY-GENERATED LEADS.

MAIL

MEETING NEW PEOPLE, GETTING REFERRALS, AND MAKING APPOINTMENTS ...

BUT LET'S SUPPOSE THAT, FOR WHATEVER REASON, YOU'RE NOT READY AND WILLING TO PUT ON A STRONG PROSPECTING DRIVE RIGHT NOW.

HERE'S HOW TO HOLD THINGS TOGETHER UNTIL YOU'RE READY TO MAKE YOUR DRIVE FOR THE *BIG MONEY*.

HANDLE PROBLEMS FAST.

CALL PEOPLE BACK IMMEDIATELY.

KEEP EVERY PROMISE MADE.

KEEP IN TOUCH.

MOST CHAMPIONS MAKE SOME KIND OF CONTACT AT LEAST EVERY NINETY DAYS.

THERE ARE ALSO LEADS YOU GENERATE WHERE THERE'S NO REFERRAL INVOLVED

THEY'RE NOT PREQUALIFIED, SO YOU'LL ONLY CLOSE 10% OF THEM.

THEREFORE, YOU NEED TO LEARN HOW TO FIND NEW LEADS, BUT ALSO HOW TO **PREQUALIFY** THEM.

A LEAD IS PREQUALIFIED WHEN YOU KNOW THAT THE EMOTIONAL AND LOGICAL REQUIREMENTS FOR BENEFITING FROM YOUR PRODUCT OR SERVICE ARE ALL PRESENT.

THE SALE DEPENDS ON EMOTION BACKED BY LOGIC.

EMOTION COMES FIRST ...

BACKED BY *LOGIC*.

IT DOES NOT HAPPEN THE OTHER WAY AROUND.

YOU PREQUALIFY PEOPLE BY FINDING OUT WHETHER THE EMOTION THAT'S NECESSARY TO CARRY THE SALE TO COMPLETION EXISTS OR CAN BE CREATED.

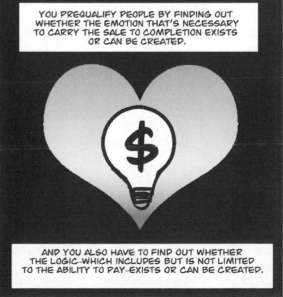

AND YOU ALSO HAVE TO FIND OUT WHETHER THE LOGIC—WHICH INCLUDES BUT IS NOT LIMITED TO THE ABILITY TO PAY—EXISTS OR CAN BE CREATED.

THERE ARE A NUMBER OF TECHNIQUES TO HELP YOU DO THIS.

FOR EXAMPLE, **THE ITCH CYCLE**. THIS IS AN EXCITING WAY TO PROSPECT, **NOT** A SKIN DISEASE.

IN REAL ESTATE, FOR EXAMPLE, THE AVERAGE TURNOVER IS 3 TO 5 YEARS. THIS MEANS THE AVERAGE FAMILY STARTS CONSIDERING MOVING EVERY FIVE YEARS OR SO.

IF YOU'RE IN AUTOMOBILE SALES, PEOPLE GET THE ITCH TO BUY A NEW CAR ABOUT EVERY 30 MONTHS.

OFFICE EQUIPMENT SALESPEOPLE KNOW THAT THE CUSTOMER CYCLE IS ABOUT EVERY THREE YEARS.

CHAMPIONS KEEP IN TOUCH WITH ALL THEIR PAST BUYERS, AND THEY START THEIR UPDATE CAMPAIGN ABOUT SIXTY DAYS BEFORE THE ITCHIEST TIME.

ORPHAN ADOPTION

WHEN SALESPEOPLE LEAVE AN ORGANIZATION, THEY LEAVE THEIR CLIENTELE BEHIND. SALES SUCCEED WHEN YOU FOLLOW UP WITH THIS CLIENTELE.

TECHNICAL ADVANCEMENT.

WE ALL WANT THE SHINIEST, NEWEST, FASTEST, HIGHEST-PERFORMANCE PRODUCTS AND SERVICES. WHEN YOU HAVE A NEW PRODUCT-OR AN OLD PRODUCT IN A NEW STYLE OR WITH A NEW FEATURE-CALL EVERYONE WHO ALREADY HAS YOUR PRODUCT.

KEEP UP WITH LOCAL NEWS.

READ ARTICLES AND NEWS ITEMS TO IDENTIFY WHERE YOUR PRODUCT OR SERVICE COULD HELP SOMEONE. CHAMPIONS READ THEIR LOCAL NEWS TO LOOK FOR WAYS TO GENERATE BUSINESS. DOZENS OF PEOPLE ADVERTISE A MESSAGE OF GREAT IMPORTANCE EVERY DAY: WE NEED YOUR HELP.

CLAIM STAKING.

MAKE YOURSELF KNOWN WITHIN A COMPANY OR ORGANIZATION AS SOMEONE DEDICATED TO SERVING THE NEEDS OF OTHERS. DON'T RELY ON A SINGLE CONTACT PERSON FOR BUSINESS.

START WORKING SOME TARGET COMPANIES RIGHT NOW-BEFORE THE NEW PEOPLE WHO'LL GET PUBLICITY ARRIVE! THEN, WHEN THEY SHOW UP, YOU'LL BE AN INSIDER AND GET FIRST CRACK AT THEM.

SWAP MEETS AND LEAD CLUBS.

THE IDEA HERE IS TO MEET REGULARLY TO SWAP LEADS WITH CAREFULLY SELECTED SALESPEOPLE WHO SELL IN A NONCOMPETING FIELD.

COMMUNITY INVOLVEMENT.

IF YOU WANT TO REACH PEOPLE LIVING IN A CERTAIN GEOGRAPHIC LOCATION, CONSIDER GETTING INVOLVED IN COMMUNITY EVENTS.

25

THE **REFERRED LEAD**, THOUGH, IS THE EASIEST TO CLOSE.

CHAMPIONS CLOSE REFERRALS TWICE AS FAST AS THEY CLOSE NON-REFERRED PROSPECTS.

EVEN MORE EXCITING IS THE FACT THAT CHAMPIONS WILL CLOSE 40 TO 60 PERCENT OF THEIR QUALIFIED REFERRALS.

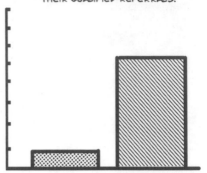

NON-REFERRED LEADS   QUALIFIED REFERRALS

LET ME SHOW YOU WHAT CHAMPIONS DO. ONCE YOU MASTER THIS, YOU'RE GOING TO GET QUALIFIED LEADS AFTER EVERY SALE.

YOU HAVE TO USE THIS TECHNIQUE IN A CASUAL, **NON-THREATENING** WAY. THE PROCESS BEGINS AS SOON AS YOU MEET PEOPLE.

DURING YOUR INITIAL CONVERSATION, YOU MUST LOOK FOR CLUES AS TO THE SMALL GROUPS OF PEOPLE YOUR CONTACT MIGHT KNOW.

JOHN, THE REASON MY COMPANY DOESN'T SPEND MILLIONS ON ADVERTISING IS BECAUSE WE'VE CHOSEN TO BUILD OUR BUSINESS ON WORD-OF-MOUTH RECOMMENDATIONS.

WHEN I HAVE SATISFIED YOUR NEEDS WITH THIS PRODUCT AND YOU ARE THRILLED WITH MY COMPANY, WOULD YOU HAVE ANY CHALLENGES WITH ME ASKING FOR AN INTRODUCTION TO A FEW OTHER PEOPLE I MIGHT SERVE?

AFTER THE SALE IS MADE, IT'S TIME TO REMIND THEM ABOUT THEIR AGREEMENT.

JOHN, DO YOU REMEMBER WHEN WE FIRST TALKED, I ASKED IF YOU'D MIND GIVING ME THE NAMES OF A FEW OTHER PEOPLE TO SERVE?

CAN WE COME UP WITH ANYONE ELSE YOU KNOW WHO MIGHT HAVE A NEED FOR OR ENJOY THE SAME BENEFITS YOU ARE EXCITED ABOUT? PERHAPS ONE OF YOUR FISHING BUDDIES? BUSINESS ASSOCIATES?

THE TELEPHONE IS YOUR SECOND MOST IMPORTANT SELLING TOOL— THE FIRST BEING YOUR MOUTH. YET, FOR REASONS THAT ESCAPE ME, FEW SALESPEOPLE REALLY STUDY THE TECHNIQUES OF THE TELEPHONE.

THE WORST MISCONCEPTION THE AVERAGE SALESPERSON HAS ABOUT THE TELEPHONE IS THE IDEA THAT A TELEPHONE CAN SUBSTITUTE FOR A FACE-TO-FACE MEETING WITH THE PROSPECT.

UNLESS YOU ARE IN TELEMARKETING YOU **MUST** MEET ALL QUALIFIED, INTERESTED CALLERS IN **PERSON**.

LET ME GIVE YOU SOME BASIC TIPS ON HOW TO USE THE TELEPHONE TO GENERATE MONEY, NOT TROUBLE.

ALWAYS BE COURTEOUS, AND HANDLE CALLS IMMEDIATELY.

ABOVE ALL, DO ANYTHING TO MEET THE CALLER. IF YOU ANSWER ALL THEIR QUESTIONS OVER THE PHONE, WHY DO THEY NEED TO MEET YOU? IF YOU DON'T MEET THEM, YOU WON'T SELL THEM.

WHERE ARE YOU NOW?

CAN YOU HOLD ON JUST A MINUTE?

OH, I JUST STOPPED IN A LITTLE COFFEE SHOP ON FIFTH STREET.

MAP WEB

THE PEOPLE WHO TRY THE HARDEST TO KEEP FROM MEETING YOU ARE OFTEN THE EASIEST ONES TO CLOSE. THAT'S WHY YOUR GOAL HAS TO BE TO MEET FACE-TO-FACE WITH CALLERS.

OF ALL THE THINGS BUYING IS, IT IS *NOT* A SPECTATOR SPORT.

APATHY RUSHES IN WHERE INVOLVEMENT FAILS TO TREAD. BUYING IS ACTION. IT CAN'T TAKE PLACE WHERE THERE ARE NO DECISIONS, AND DECISIONS CAN'T BE MADE BY A SWITCHED-OFF MIND.

WATCHING INSTEAD OF DOING CAUSES BUYERS TO SWITCH OFF, AND THE LONGER THEY ARE SWITCHED OFF, THE HARDER IT IS TO SWITCH THEM ON AGAIN.

YOU WIN THE OOOHS AND AAAAHS BY SHOWING YOUR PROSPECTS HOW TO DO AMAZING THINGS WITH YOUR PRODUCT OR SERVICE, NOT BY DOING AMAZING THINGS YOURSELF.

HERE'S HOW TO DEVELOP A CLIENT-PARTICIPATION DEMONSTRATION TECHNIQUE INTO A POWERFUL SELLING TOOL .

LIST ALL THE STEPS THE UNINITIATED MUST GO THROUGH TO UNDERSTAND HOW MUCH THEY NEED YOUR DEVICE'S CAPABILITIES. THEN FIGURE OUT AS SIMPLE AN EXERCISE AS YOU CAN TO DEMONSTRATE THE CAPABILITY.

LIST EVERY QUESTION AND OBJECTION THAT YOU'RE LIKELY TO ENCOUNTER.

STEP 1 - DISCUSS THE BENEFITS

STEP 2 - HAVE THE CLIENT USE THE WEBSITE TO PLACE AN ORDER

STEP 3 - ADDRESS THE FIREWALL ISSUE AS THEY LOG-ON

STEP 4 ....

ARRANGE THE CAPABILITY DEMONSTRATION AND THE QUESTION/OBJECTION ANSWERING INTO A SMOOTH-FLOWING SEQUENCE.

PRACTICE YOUR NEW TECHNIQUE ON ANYONE YOU CAN.

NOW WE'RE GETTING INTO THE AREA YOU PROBABLY ENJOY MOST—WORKING FACE-TO-FACE WITH BUYERS.

UNLESS I MISS MY GUESS, YOU'RE PROBABLY GOOD AT THIS ... AND YOU PROBABLY SPEND TOO MUCH TIME ON IT.

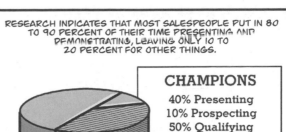

RESEARCH INDICATES THAT MOST SALESPEOPLE PUT IN 80 TO 90 PERCENT OF THEIR TIME PRESENTING AND DEMONSTRATING, LEAVING ONLY 10 TO 20 PERCENT FOR OTHER THINGS.

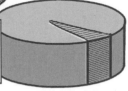

CHAMPIONS
40% Presenting
10% Prospecting
50% Qualifying & planning

EVERYONE ELSE
90% Demonstrating
10% Everything else

CHAMPIONS, ON THE OTHER HAND, SPEND ONLY 40 PERCENT OF THEIR TIME PRESENTING, NO MORE THAN 10 PERCENT PROSPECTING, AND ABOUT 50 PERCENT QUALIFYING AND PLANNING. AND CHAMPIONS CLOSE A FAR HIGHER PERCENTAGE OF THE PEOPLE THEY PRESENT TO THAN THE NON-CHAMPIONS.

IF YOU WANT TO MAKE A HALF-HOUR SPEECH, YOU SHOULD REALLY WRITE A TEN-MINUTE SPEECH.

WHY?

IF YOU'RE GOING TO GET YOUR POINT ACROSS, YOU MUST FOLLOW THESE STEPS ...

TELL THEM WHAT YOU'RE GOING TO TELL THEM.

TELL THEM WHAT YOU'RE THERE TO TELL THEM.

TELL THEM WHAT YOU JUST TOLD THEM.

IN OTHER WORDS, WE USE *REPETITION*.

WE DON'T SAY EXACTLY THE SAME THING THREE TIMES OF COURSE. IN THE FIRST 10 MINUTES, WE'RE INTRODUCING OUR NEW IDEAS. IN THE SECOND 10 MINUTES, WE'RE COVERING THE POINTS IN DEPTH AND RELATING THEM TO OUR LISTENERS' INTERESTS AND NEEDS.

IN THE LAST 10 MINUTES, WE'RE DRAWING CONCLUSIONS AND INDICATING THE DIRECTION THAT THEY SHOULD TAKE.

A CHAMPION SPEAKS TO A PLUMBER IN A PLUMBER'S LANGUAGE AND TO A DOCTOR IN A DOCTOR'S LANGUAGE.

THE CHAMPION LEARNS TO SPEAK MANY LANGUAGES BECAUSE IT'S THE MOST EFFICIENT WAY TO ESTABLISH *RAPPORT* WITH DIFFERENT GROUPS OF PEOPLE.

DURING YOUR PRESENTATIONS, KEEP CLIENTS MENTALLY AND PHYSICALLY INVOLVED. YOU DO THIS BY ASKING INVOLVEMENT QUESTIONS THAT WILL KEEP THEM THINKING ABOUT HOW THEY'LL USE YOUR OFFERING ONCE THEY OWN IT.

YOU MAY NOT BELIEVE THIS IS POSSIBLE, BUT YOU SHOULD GIVE THE ENTIRE BODY OF YOUR PRESENTATION IN *LESS THAN 17 MINUTES.*

KEEP THE PRESENTATION SHORT AND SWEET OR THE FINE CUTTING EDGE OF THE CLIENT'S DECISION-MAKING ABILITY WILL BE DULLED.

YOU CAN DO THIS IF YOU RIGOROUSLY CHOP OFF UNNECESSARY DETAIL, IF YOU'LL STREAMLINE WHAT YOU HAVE TO SAY, IF YOU ELIMINATE ANYTHING YOU'RE NOT POSITIVE IS CONTRIBUTING TO THE CLOSE.

VISUAL AIDS GIVE YOU CONTROL AND ALLOW FOR SPEED.

BUT LET ME WARN YOU ABOUT SOMETHING. SOME SALESPEOPLE HAVE BEAT UP OLD BINDERS THAT THEY USE FOR EVERY PRESENTATION. INSTEAD OF WORKING SMOOTHLY, THEY SPEND HALF THEIR TIME FLIPPING OVER PAGES AND MUTTERING THINGS LIKE ...

YOU AREN'T INTERESTED IN THAT.

WE DON'T HAVE THAT MODEL ANYMORE BECAUSE IT WAS A MAINTENANCE NIGHTMARE.

WHERE'S THAT SCHEMATIC I WANT TO SHOW YOU?

YOU MAY SAY, "BUT I HAVE SO MANY PRODUCTS, I HAVE TO USE THE SAME BINDER FOR ALL MY PRESENTATIONS."

BALONEY.

GOOD VISUAL AIDS EMPLOY PSYCHOLOGICAL METHODS TO CONVINCE PROSPECTS ON BOTH THE EMOTIONAL AND LOGICAL LEVEL.

VISUAL AIDS TELL THEM WHO YOU ARE. MANY PEOPLE FEEL THAT ALL SALESPEOPLE AND COMPANIES ARE ABOUT THE SAME. YOU SHOULD BE PROUD OF YOUR COMPANY, AND HERE'S THE TIME TO LET IT SHOW.

VISUAL AIDS TELL THEM WHAT YOU'VE DONE.

Goolge

MOTOR DARLEY HAVERSON BIKES

STAR BUNKS TEAS

BIM

VISUAL AIDS TELL THEM WHAT YOU'RE GOING TO DO FOR THEM.

THE FIRST IMPRESSION YOU MAKE WITH POTENTIAL CLIENTS WILL MAKE OR BREAK YOUR CHANCES OF SERVING THEM TODAY FOR AND MANY YEARS DOWN THE ROAD.

OUR MAIN GOAL WHEN FIRST MEETING A PERSON IS TO REMOVE FEAR AND ALLOW THEM TO RELAX.

IF THE DOMINANT MOOD IN THEIR MINDS IS FEAR—THAT YOU'LL PUSH THEM—THEY SIMPLY AREN'T CAPABLE OF MAKING THE KIND OF POSITIVE DECISION YOU'RE LOOKING FOR.

WHEN MEETING A POTENTIAL CLIENT, SMILE ... LOOK IN THEIR EYES ... AND GREET THEM PROPERLY.

PRACTICE AT LEAST THREE DIFFERENT GREETINGS.

TO SHAKE ... OR NOT TO SHAKE? THAT IS THE QUESTION.

FOR STARTERS YOU MAY NEED A FORMAL, RESPECTFUL GREETING; A FRIENDLY GREETING; AND A HAPPY-GO-LUCKY GREETING.

MANY AVERAGE SALESPEOPLE CAN'T WAIT TO RUSH FORWARD AND SHAKE EVERYONE'S HANDS ... BUT MANY PEOPLE DON'T WANT TO BE TOUCHED BY STRANGERS.

SIMPLY LET THE PROSPECTS DETERMINE IF THEY WANT TO SHAKE HANDS OR NOT.

THE MOST VALUABLE THING A SALESPERSON HAS IS TIME. TIME WASTED DEMONSTRATING TO NON-BUYERS IS TIME THAT COULD HAVE BEEN SPENT DEMONSTRATING TO AND CLOSING BUYERS— OR AT LEAST PROSPECTING FOR THEM.

I CALL THIS MY **NEADS QUALIFICATION SEQUENCE.** YOU MUST DETERMINE YOUR CLIENT'S NEEDS BEFORE KNOWING HOW TO PROCEED WITH THEM. I JUST SPELL IT DIFFERENTLY TO MATCH THE SEQUENCE OF QUESTIONS YOU'RE GOING TO ASK.

A NEEDS

FIND OUT WHAT THEY HAVE NOW. THE N IN NEADS STANDS FOR "*NOW*."

FIND OUT WHAT THEY LIKE MOST ABOUT THE PRODUCT OR SERVICE THEY NOW HAVE. THE E IN NEADS STANDS FOR "*ENJOY*."

"WHAT WOULD YOU LIKE TO SEE ALTERED OR IMPROVED IN YOUR NEW PRODUCT OR SERVICE?" THE A IN NEADS STANDS FOR "*ALTER*."

"WHO IN ADDITION TO YOURSELF WILL MAKE THE FINAL DECISION?"

THE D IN NEADS IS TO REMIND YOU TO BE CERTAIN YOU'RE TALKING WITH THE REAL "*DECISION MAKER*."

"IF WE WERE FORTUNATE ENOUGH TODAY TO FIND THE RIGHT SOLUTION FOR YOUR NEEDS WOULD YOU BE IN A POSITION TO PROCEED?"

THE S IN NEADS STANDS FOR "*SOLUTION*."

INSTEAD OF TRYING TO GO FROM EIGHT POSSIBILITIES TO THE ONE MACHINE PROSPECTS WILL BUY, FRAME THEM IN TO THE **MOST LIKELY THREE** FIRST.

USE THE TRIPLICATE OF CHOICE FOR MONEY, TOO.

MOST PEOPLE INTERESTED IN ACQUIRING THIS MACHINE WITH ALL ITS FEATURES ARE PREPARED TO INVEST $12,000. A FORTUNATE FEW CAN INVEST BETWEEN $15,000 AND $20,000.

AND THEN THERE ARE THOSE ON A LIMITED OR FIXED BUDGET WHO—WITH THE HIGH COST OF EVERYTHING TODAY—CAN'T GO HIGHER THAN $10,000.

WHICH OF THESE CATEGORIES DOES YOUR COMPANY FIT INTO MOST COMFORTABLY?

TO USE THE TRIPLICATE OF CHOICE FOR MONEY YOU MUST PRACTICE THE FIGURES UNTIL YOU KNOW THEM PERFECTLY.

OBJECTIONS ARE THE RUNGS OF THE LADDER TO SALES SUCCESS.

THERE ARE TWO KINDS OF OBJECTIONS, MINOR AND MAJOR.

MINOR OBJECTIONS ARE DEFENSE MECHANISMS.

PEOPLE USE THEM TO SLOW THINGS DOWN. THEY DON'T MEAN THAT THEY DON'T WANT TO BUY; THEY MAY NEED ADDITIONAL INFORMATION BEFORE COMMITTING THEMSELVES.

THEY'LL TOSS OBJECTIONS AT YOU ALL DAY LONG IF YOU ALLOW IT.

THERE ARE TWO DON'TS AND ONE DO THAT EVERY CHAMPION LIVES BY WHEN IT COMES TO OBJECTIONS.

DON'T ARGUE.

DON'T ATTACK YOUR CLIENT WHEN YOU OVERCOME THEIR OBJECTIONS.

DO LEAD YOUR CLIENT TO ANSWER THEIR OWN OBJECTIONS.

HERE'S A GOOD OBJECTION HANDLING SYSTEM.

HEAR THEM OUT. FEED THE OBJECTION BACK. QUESTION THE CONCERN. ANSWER THE OBJECTION. CONFIRM THE ANSWER.

CHANGE GEARS, AND IMMEDIATELY GO TO THE NEXT STEP IN YOUR SELLING SEQUENCE OR ONTO THE NEXT OBJECTION OR CONCERN RAISED.

I'M GIVING YOU LOTS OF TECHNIQUES FOR PROSPECTING, MEETING PEOPLE, BUILDING A FULL LIST OF REFERRALS, QUALIFYING, PRESENTING, DEMONSTRATING, AND OVERCOMING OBJECTIONS, AND THEY'RE ALL IMPORTANT.

BUT IT'S NO GOOD IF YOU PLAY YOUR WHOLE GAME IN YOUR OWN TERRITORY AND NEVER GET ACROSS THE GOAL LINE.

SO WELCOME TO THE DELIGHTFUL WORLD OF *CLOSING*. IF YOU DON'T LOVE IT NOW, START FALLING IN LOVE, BECAUSE THIS IS WHERE THE MONEY IS.

FIRST, LET'S DISCUSS SOME SPECIFIC CLOSING TIPS.

ALWAYS HAVE YOUR CLOSING MATERIALS WITH YOU. BE READY TO CLOSE ANYTIME AND ANYWHERE.

A SUPPLY OF CLOSING MATERIAL SHOULD TAKE UP A PERMANENT RESIDENCE IN YOUR BRIEFCASE, CLUB LOCKER, OVERNIGHT BAG, CAR—AND LET'S NOT OVERLOOK YOUR OFFICE DESK.

WORK CLEAN.

USE CRISP NEW FORMS, NOT THE ONES YOU SPILLED COFFEE ON.

FIND FIGURES WITH FINESSE.

CHAMPIONS DO THEIR SELLING ARITHMETIC WITH A CALCULATOR, NOT A PENCIL.

MAKE YOUR PROOF LETTERS TALK.

THIS SERVICE IS AMAZING!

PROOF OR TESTIMONIAL LETTERS ARE POWERFUL TOOLS TO HELP PEOPLE GET INVOLVED. THE IMPORTANT THING TO REMEMBER HERE IS THAT THE MOST POWERFUL LETTERS ARE THOSE FROM PEOPLE KNOWN TO YOUR PROSPECTS.

THE DEFINITION OF CLOSING IS PROFESSIONALLY USING PEOPLE'S DESIRE TO OWN THE BENEFITS OF YOUR PRODUCT. THEN, BLENDING YOUR SINCERE DESIRE TO SERVE IN HELPING THEM MAKE DECISIONS THAT ARE TRULY GOOD FOR THEM.

THE REASON SO MANY PEOPLE NEED HELP IN MAKING DECISIONS IS THAT THEY'RE AFRAID OF MAKING BAD ONES. INDECISION IS ONE OF THE GREAT DESTROYERS, IT DRIVES A FEW PEOPLE CRAZY, AND SAPS THE ENERGY OUT OF MOST OF US.

HERO'S WAY OUT

COWARD'S WAY OUT

INSECURITY CAUSES PROCRASTINATION, AND THAT LEADS TO INDECISION.

RATHER THAN INVOLVING PEOPLE IN INSECURITY, HELP THEM FIND THEIR OWN WAY TO OWNERSHIP.

MANY SALESPEOPLE HAVE A CHALLENGE WITH THEIR OWN LIKES AND DISLIKES. THEY ONLY SELL WHAT THEY LIKE TO THE PEOPLE THEY LIKE, AND MAKE ONLY A FRACTION OF THE BEST INCOME THEY COULD ACHIEVE.

CATER TO YOUR OWN PREFERENCES ON YOUR OWN TIME.

YOU MUST SEE THE BENEFITS, FEATURES, AND LIMITATIONS OF YOUR PRODUCT OR SERVICE FROM YOUR POTENTIAL BUYER'S VIEWPOINT.

YOU MUST WEIGH THEM ON THE BUYER'S SCALE OF VALUES, NOT YOUR OWN. CLOSE ON THE BENEFITS THAT ARE MOST VIABLE TO YOUR BUYER.

THERE'S A CERTAIN ELECTRICITY IN THE AIR WHEN YOU'RE READY TO GO AHEAD WITH YOUR CLOSE. YOU WILL WANT TO WATCH FOR THE SIGNS.

START YOUR CLOSING SEQUENCE ...

...WHEN THEY'VE BEEN COMING ALONG AT A CERTAIN PACE, AND SUDDENLY THEY SLOW THE PACE DOWN.

... OR WHEN THEY SUDDENLY SPEED THAT PACE UP.

... WHEN THEY'VE MOSTLY BEEN LISTENING, AND SUDDENLY THEY START ASKING A LOT OF QUESTIONS.

... WHEN THEY GIVE YOU POSITIVE STIMULI AT THE RIGHT TIME.

BE READY TO CLOSE ANYWHERE, ANYTIME.

MOST SALES ARE MADE ON THE HOODS OF CARS, IN RESTAURANTS, ON THE CUSTOMER'S DESK, STANDING IN DISPLAY ROOMS, ON KITCHEN TABLES, AND COUNTLESS OTHER PLACES THAT ARE NOT DESIGNED PRIMARILY FOR CLOSING BUSINESS.

HERE ARE THE 16 MOST IMPORTANT WORDS IN THE ART OF CLOSING.

WHENEVER YOU ASK A CLOSING QUESTION, **SHUT UP.** THE FIRST PERSON TO SPEAK OWNS THE PRODUCT.

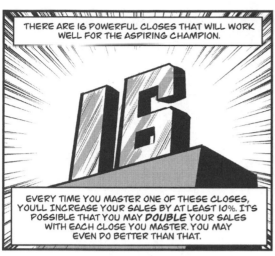

THERE ARE 16 POWERFUL CLOSES THAT WILL WORK WELL FOR THE ASPIRING CHAMPION.

EVERY TIME YOU MASTER ONE OF THESE CLOSES, YOU'LL INCREASE YOUR SALES BY AT LEAST 10%. IT'S POSSIBLE THAT YOU MAY *DOUBLE* YOUR SALES WITH EACH CLOSE YOU MASTER. YOU MAY EVEN DO BETTER THAN THAT.

THE BASIC ORAL CLOSE.

THIS IS PRIMARILY FOR INDUSTRIAL, COMMERCIAL, AND GOVERNMENTAL SALES.

BY THE WAY, WHAT PURCHASE ORDER NUMBER WILL BE ASSIGNED TO THIS REQUISITION?

THE BASIC, WRITTEN CLOSE A.K.A. THE "LET ME MAKE A NOTE OF THAT" CLOSE.

THIS IS AN EFFECTIVE CLOSE IF YOU USE AN ORDER FORM.

YOU SAY YOU WOULD NEED DELIVERY NO LATER THAN THE 15TH? LET ME MAKE A NOTE OF THAT.

THE BENJAMIN FRANKLIN BALANCE SHEET CLOSE.

THIS CLOSE IS BASED ON THE ACTUAL WAY BENJAMIN FRANKLIN ARRIVED AT DECISIONS, AND MUCH OF ITS PERSUASIVENESS COMES FROM OUR RESPECT FOR HIS NAME.

AS YOU KNOW, WE AMERICANS HAVE LONG CONSIDERED BENJAMIN FRANKLIN ONE OF OUR WISEST MEN. WHENEVER OLD BEN FOUND HIMSELF IN A SITUATION SUCH AS YOU'RE IN TODAY, HE FELT PRETTY MUCH AS YOU DO ABOUT IT.

IF IT WAS THE RIGHT THING, HE WANTED TO BE SURE TO DO IT. IF IT WAS THE WRONG THING, HE WANTED TO BE SURE TO AVOID IT. ISN'T THAT ABOUT THE WAY YOU FEEL?

HERE'S WHAT OLD BEN WOULD DO. HE'D TAKE A SHEET OF PAPER AND DRAW A LINE DOWN THE MIDDLE. ON ONE SIDE OF THE SHEET HE WROTE "YES," AND UNDER THAT HE'D NOTE ALL THE REASONS FAVORING THE DECISION.

THEN, UNDER "NO," HE'D LIST ALL THE REASONS AGAINST THE DECISION. WHEN HE WAS THROUGH HE SIMPLY COUNTED THE PROS AND CONS, AND THE DECISION WAS MADE FOR HIM. LET'S TRY IT, OKAY?

YES   NO

THE "I WANT TO THINK IT OVER" CLOSE.

NEARLY ALL OF YOUR POTENTIAL CLIENTS WILL TRY TO SLOW THINGS DOWN BY MAKING ONE OF THE FOLLOWING STATEMENTS.

I WANT TO THINK IT OVER.

I WANT TO SLEEP ON IT.

I DON'T JUMP INTO THINGS.

WHEN YOU HEAR ANY OF THOSE LINES AFTER YOU'VE LEARNED THIS CLOSE, YOU'LL THINK ...

I OWN THIS ...

HERE'S WHAT THE CHAMPION DOES WHEN THE CLIENT PLAYS THE "I WANT TO THINK IT OVER" NUMBER.

AGREE WITH THEM. CONFIRM THE FACT THAT THEY'RE GOING TO THINK IT OVER. CLARIFY AND ASK AGAIN.

JUST TO CLARIFY MY THINKING, WHAT IS IT THAT YOU WANTED TO THINK OVER IS IT THE INTEGRITY OF MY COMPANY?

NOTICE THAT I RAN THOSE TWO SENTENCES TOGETHER. REMEMBER THAT PAUSING BETWEEN "OVER" AND "IS" IS OFTEN PURE DISASTER. DON'T TURN THIS MOST IMPORTANT ELEMENT OF THE CLOSE INTO TWO SENTENCES.

IS IT THE LEVEL OF SERVICE I'LL PROVIDE? IS IT THE PRODUCT'S CAPABILITIES?

IS IT THE QUALITY OF THE PRODUCT?

ASK QUESTIONS THAT'LL CAUSE THEM TO TELL YOU HOW GREAT YOUR PRODUCT IS. THERE'S NO BETTER WAY TO CONVINCE THEM OF ITS MERITS.

USUALLY, THIS BOILS DOWN TO THE MONEY.

CONFIRM THAT IT'S THE MONEY. YOU'VE GOT TO MAKE SURE THAT YOU'RE NOT DANCING WITH PHANTOMS ANYMORE. THERE'S NO POINT IN TRYING TO CLOSE ON THE MONEY ISSUE IF YOU AREN'T SURE THEY'D BUY EVEN IF IT WAS A WISE MONEY DECISION FOR THEM.

THE REDUCTION TO THE RIDICULOUS CLOSE.

HAVE YOU EVER HEARD, "IT'S HIGHER THAN WE WANTED TO GO?" I HAVE, HUNDREDS OF TIMES. AND I NEVER SOLD MUCH UNTIL I LEARNED HOW TO TURN THIS STALL INTO A CLOSE.

THE FIRST STEP IS TO FIND OUT HOW MUCH "TOO MUCH" IT IS.

IT'S *$2000* MORE THAN I WANT TO PAY

LET'S JUST SAY THAT, HYPOTHETICALLY, YOU OWN THE *SUPERPOW COPIER*. DO YOU THINK YOU'LL KEEP IT FOR FIVE YEARS?

IF WE DIVIDE $2,000 BY FIVE YEARS IT'S ONLY $400 A YEAR. NOW, YOUR COMPANY WILL USE THE SUPERPOW ALL THE TIME, RIGHT? IF WE DIVIDE THAT $400 BY 12 MONTHS, THAT'S ONLY $33.34 A MONTH OR $7.69 A WEEK.

I UNDERSTAND THAT THERE'S A LOT OF WEEKEND WORK IN THIS OFFICE, A LOT OF OVERTIME. SO IT'S REASONABLE TO SAY YOUR COPIER WOULD BE IN USE SIX DAYS A WEEK. DIVIDING EIGHT DOLLARS BY 6 DAYS WE GET ... $1.28.

DO YOU THINK WE SHOULD LET $1.28 A DAY STAND BETWEEN YOUR COMPANY AND THE PROFITS, THE INCREASED PRODUCTION, AND THE EXPANDED CAPABILITIES THE SUPERPOW WILL BRING YOU?

$1.28

LET ME ASK YOU ONE MORE THING. WOULD THIS HIGH-SPEED MACHINE WITH ALL THE SOPHISTICATED CAPABILITIES AND TIME-SAVING FEATURES MAKE MORE PROFIT FOR YOUR COMPANY IN A DAY THAN A CLERK CAN IN 20 MINUTES?

YES.

THEN WE'VE AGREED, HAVEN'T WE? BY THE WAY WHICH DELIVERY DATE WOULD BEST SUIT YOUR TIME AND SCHEDULE?

ORDER FORM

THE SHARP ANGLE CLOSE.

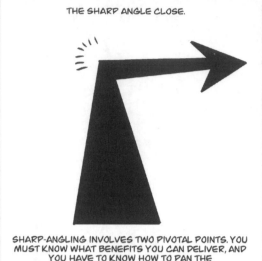

SHARP-ANGLING INVOLVES TWO PIVOTAL POINTS. YOU MUST KNOW WHAT BENEFITS YOU CAN DELIVER, AND YOU HAVE TO KNOW HOW TO PAN THE GOLD FROM THAT INFORMATION.

IF I DECIDED TO BUY THIS TV, I'D HAVE TO TAKE DELIVERY BEFORE THE BIG GAME ...

IF I COULD GUARANTEE DELIVERY BEFORE THE GAME, ARE YOU PREPARED TO MAKE THE PURCHASE TODAY?

THE SECONDARY QUESTION CLOSE.

WHEN USED AT THE RIGHT MOMENT, WITH THE RIGHT PEOPLE, THIS CLOSE IS EXCELLENT!

AS I SEE IT, MARILYN, THE ONLY DECISION WE HAVE TO MAKE TODAY IS HOW SOON YOU'LL START ENJOYING THE INCREASED PROFITS THAT A HAPPIER STAFF WILL MAKE FOR YOU—

BY THE WAY, ARE YOU GOING TO PIPE MUSIC INTO YOUR OFFICES AND WAREHOUSE ONLY, OR TO THE ENTIRE PLANT?

YOU POSE THE MAJOR DECISION AS A QUESTION, THEN IMMEDIATELY FOLLOW IT WITH ANOTHER "SECONDARY" QUESTION. TO USE THIS CLOSE SUCCESSFULLY, YOU MUST STATE THE DECISION IN TERMS OF A BENEFIT TO THE CLIENT.

AVOID ANY PAUSE BETWEEN POSING THE MAJOR DECISION AND ASKING THE SECONDARY QUESTION.

STATE THE SECONDARY QUESTION IN TERMS THAT INDICATE A CHOICE OF ANSWERS, ALL OF WHICH CONFIRM THEY ARE GOING AHEAD.

MY DEAR OLD MOTHER CLOSE.

THIS IS A CUTE ONE THAT, IN THE RIGHT CIRCUMSTANCES, WILL REALLY SHAKE THE APPLES OUT OF THE TREE. IMAGINE YOU'RE PRACTICING THE WISE ADVICE OF SHUTTING UP AFTER ASKING A CLOSING QUESTION, BUT NO ONE ELSE IS TALKING EITHER.

IF YOU FEEL YOU MUST SPEAK, SAY,

MY DEAR OLD MOTHER ONCE SAID, 'SILENCE MEANS CONSENT.' WAS SHE RIGHT?

THIS IS A MINOR TECHNIQUE THAT BREAKS THE TENSION.

THE PUPPY DOG CLOSE.

WITH THIS TECHNIQUE, YOU SELL YOUR PRODUCT JUST LIKE YOU WOULD A PUPPY DOG. HOW DO YOU SELL A PUPPY? YOU LET THE CLIENT TAKE IT HOME.

THE SIMILAR SITUATION CLOSE.

WHEN YOU FIND YOURSELF WORKING WITH SOMEONE WHO HAS A CONCERN SIMILAR TO ONE YOU'VE JUST OVERCOME, YOU CAN SHARE THE STORY.

THE "IT ISN'T IN THE BUDGET" CLOSE.

WHEN YOU'RE WORKING WITH A PRESIDENT, CFO, OR COO AND YOU ENCOUNTER THIS RESISTANCE, RESPOND IN A CORDIAL MANNER.

OF COURSE, I UNDERSTAND THIS ISN'T IN THE BUDGET.

THAT'S WHY I CAME TO YOU. I KNOW THAT EVERY WELL-MANAGED COMPANY CONTROLS ITS MONEY CAREFULLY WITH A BUDGET. I'M ALSO ASSUMING THAT A CHIEF EXECUTIVE OFFICER SUCH AS YOURSELF USES THAT BUDGET AS A GUIDELINE, NOT AN INFLEXIBLE ANCHOR.

YOU, AS THE CHIEF EXECUTIVE OFFICER, RESERVE THE RIGHT TO FLEX THE BUDGET IN THE INTERESTS OF THE COMPANY'S FINANCIAL AND COMPETITIVE FUTURE. ISN'T THAT RIGHT?

CONTRA

THE ECONOMIC TRUTH CLOSE.

IT'S NOT ALWAYS WISE TO MAKE BUYING DECISIONS BY PRICE ALONE. INVESTING TOO LITTLE HAS DRAWBACKS. YOU RISK THAT THE ITEM YOU'VE PURCHASED MAY NOT GIVE YOU THE SATISFACTION YOU WERE EXPECTING.

IT'S AN ECONOMIC TRUTH THAT IT'S SELDOM POSSIBLE TO GET THE MOST BY SPENDING THE LEAST. IT MIGHT BE WISE TO ADD A LITTLE TO YOUR INVESTMENT TO COVER THE RISK YOU'RE TAKING, WOULDN'T IT?

LET'S SAY YOU HAVE A SUPERIOR PRODUCT, BUT YOU RUN UP AGAINST A COMPETITOR WITH A LESS EXPENSIVE, YET INFERIOR PRODUCT. TRY THIS.

THE "I CAN GET IT CHEAPER" CLOSE.

I CAN GET THIS CHEAPER SOMEWHERE ELSE.

SAME DAY INSTALL AND SERVICE

THAT MAY BE TRUE. AND, AFTER ALL, IN TODAY'S ECONOMY, WE ALL WANT THE MOST FOR OUR MONEY. A TRUTH I'VE LEARNED OVER THE YEARS IS THAT THE CHEAPEST PRICE IS NOT ALWAYS WHAT WE WANT.

MOST PEOPLE LOOK FOR THREE THINGS WHEN MAKING AN INVESTMENT: QUALITY, SERVICE, AND LOWEST PRICE.

I HAVE NEVER FOUND A COMPANY THAT COULD PROVIDE THE FINEST QUALITY AND BEST SERVICE AT THE LOWEST PRICE. I'M CURIOUS. FOR YOUR LONG-TERM HAPPINESS, WHICH OF THE THREE WOULD YOU BE MOST WILLING TO GIVE UP?

THE COMPETITIVE EDGE CLOSE.

PLEASE REALIZE THAT MANY OF YOUR COMPETITORS ARE FACING THE SAME ISSUES AND CHALLENGES AS YOU.

ISN'T IT INTERESTING THAT WHEN MANY COMPANIES ARE FACING THE SAME CHALLENGES, SOME DO A BETTER JOB THAN OTHERS? MY OBJECTIVE HAS BEEN TO PROVIDE YOU WITH A METHOD FOR GAINING A COMPETITIVE EDGE. AND GAINING EDGES—LARGE AND SMALL—IS HOW YOU CAN MAKE THIS ONE OF THE FEW COMPANIES IN YOUR INDUSTRY DOING A BETTER JOB.

THE HIGHER AUTHORITY CLOSE.

IF YOU'RE SELLING WELDING EQUIPMENT AND ONE OF YOUR CLIENTS IS A TOP STEEL FABRICATOR, THEIR PRODUCTION MANAGER MIGHT BE A GREAT CHOICE FOR AN EXPERT IN THE EYES OF SMALLER STEEL FABRICATORS.

TO USE THIS CLOSE EFFECTIVELY, YOU MUST ...

THANKS FOR COMING MARK!

RECRUIT YOUR HIGHER AUTHORITY FIGURE.

ASK YOUR EXPERT IF HE WOULD BE WILLING TO SHARE HIS KNOWLEDGE OF YOUR PRODUCT WITH OTHER NON-COMPETING STEEL FABRICATORS.

PROJECT COST REPORT

SET YOUR HIGHER AUTHORITY FIGURE UP FOR THE SPECIFIC SALES SITUATION.

ONCE YOU HAVE A LIST OF QUESTIONS, CONCERNS, OR OBJECTIONS YOUR CLIENT MIGHT BE EXPERIENCING, ASK ...

YOU KNOW MARK CADE, DON'T YOU? HE'S ONE OF OUR CLIENTS.

THEN MAKE A QUICK PHONE CALL AND HAVE YOUR EXPERT GO OVER THE QUESTIONS WITH THE CLIENT.

MARK CADE

THE LOST SALE CLOSE.

IF YOU'VE DONE **EVERYTHING** YOU CAN AND YOU STILL FEEL YOUR PRODUCT IS RIGHT FOR YOUR CLIENT, GIVE IT ONE MORE SHOT.

PARDON ME, MR. AND MRS. SMITH, BUT BEFORE I LEAVE, MAY I APOLOGIZE FOR NOT DOING MY JOB TODAY?

YOU SEE, IF I HAD NOT BEEN INEPT, I WOULD HAVE SAID THE THINGS NECESSARY TO CONVINCE YOU OF THE VALUE OF MY PRODUCT. I DIDN'T, AND YOU WILL NOT BE ENJOYING THE BENEFITS OF OUR PRODUCT.

AND BELIEVE ME, I AM TRULY SORRY. SO THAT I DON'T MAKE THE SAME MISTAKE AGAIN, COULD YOU TELL ME WHAT I DID WRONG? AND PLEASE BE CANDID WITH ME.

IF YOU DELIVER THOSE WORDS WITH WARMTH AND SINCERITY, THE CLIENTS WILL USUALLY GIVE YOU SOMETHING YOU CAN WORK WITH.

BUT WHAT IS THE MOST VITAL SKILL FOR YOU TO CULTIVATE ON YOUR PATH TO BECOMING A CHAMPION?

Who wants to be a Champion

$5200

$2515

$7500

THE AVERAGE HUMAN BEING HAS THE ABILITY TO ACHIEVE ALMOST **ANYTHING.** LACK OF BASIC CAPABILITY IS RARELY THE CAUSE OF UNDERACHIEVEMENT.

THE CHALLENGE IS ALMOST ALWAYS IN FINDING OUT **WHAT YOU WANT.**

IF YOU REALLY WANT SOMETHING, THAT DESIRE WILL MAKE A DIFFERENCE IN YOUR LIFE. YOU'LL DO WHATEVER IT TAKES TO ACHIEVE IT. YOU'LL SACRIFICE PLEASURES AND CHANGE YOURSELF AND GROW SO THAT YOU CAN HAVE WHAT YOU WANT.

THAT'S WHY YOU MUST PUT WHAT YOU WANT ON PAPER. THEN LOOK AT YOUR GOALS, WRITTEN THERE IN BLACK AND WHITE, AND COMMIT TO THEM.

GOAL-SETTING IS THE MOST NECESSARY OF ALL SKILLS, AND SOME RULES MUST BE FOLLOWED IF THE SYSTEM IS GOING TO WORK.

IF IT'S NOT *IN WRITING*, IT'S NOT A GOAL.

IF IT'S NOT *SPECIFIC*, IT'S NOT A GOAL.

GOALS MUST BE BELIEVABLE.

WRITTEN
SPECIFIC
BELIEVABLE

AN EFFECTIVE GOAL IS AN *EXCITING CHALLENGE*.

IF YOUR GOAL DOESN'T PUSH YOU BEYOND WHERE YOU'VE BEEN BEFORE—IF IT DOESN'T DEMAND YOUR BEST AND A BIT MORE—IT ISN'T GOING TO CHANGE YOUR WAYS AND ELEVATE YOUR LIFESTYLE.

GOALS MUST BE *ADJUSTED* TO NEW INFORMATION.

SET YOUR GOALS QUICKLY, AND ADJUST THEM LATER IF YOU AIM TOO HIGH OR TOO LOW.

DYNAMIC GOALS GUIDE OUR CHOICES.

MANY DIFFERENT THINGS DEMAND OUR ATTENTION, BUT IF YOUR GOALS ARE SET UP RIGHT, THEY'LL INSTANTLY SHOW YOU THE RIGHT WAY TO GO ON MOST DECISIONS.

DON'T SET SHORT-TERM GOALS FOR MORE THAN 90 DAYS.

IF A SHORT-TERM GOAL TAKES MORE THAN 90 DAYS, YOU'LL LOSE INTEREST.

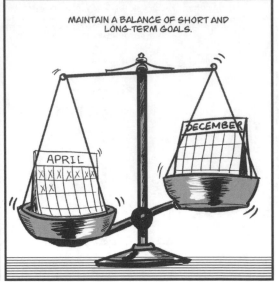

MAINTAIN A BALANCE OF SHORT AND LONG-TERM GOALS.

INCLUDE YOUR LOVED ONES IN YOUR GOALS.

SET GOALS IN **ALL AREAS** OF YOUR LIFE.

GOALS AREN'T JUST ABOUT MAKING MONEY. SET GOALS FOR HEALTH, FOR EXERCISE, FOR SPORTS, IN YOUR PERSONAL LIFE, AND IN YOUR FAMILY AND SPIRITUAL LIFE.

YOUR GOALS MUST **HARMONIZE**.

WHENEVER YOU DETECT A CONFLICT, SET PRIORITIES THAT WILL ELIMINATE THE CONFLICT.

REVIEW YOUR GOALS REGULARLY.

SET *VIVID* GOALS.

YOU WON'T STRETCH FOR THE HO-HUMS OF LIFE, WILL YOU?

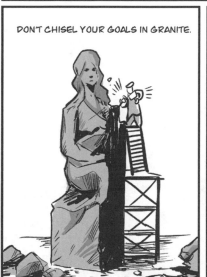

DON'T CHISEL YOUR GOALS IN GRANITE.

REACH OUT INTO THE *FUTURE.* BEGIN BY SETTING 20 YEAR GOALS.

TRAIN YOURSELF TO *CRAVE YOUR GOALS.*

SPEND TIME VISUALIZING YOURSELF POSSESSING WHAT YOU'VE SET YOUR GOAL FOR.

SET *ACTIVITY GOALS,* NOT PRODUCTION GOALS.

HOW MANY PEOPLE WILL YOU MEET TODAY? HOW MANY CALLS WILL YOU MAKE? HOW MANY PRESENTATIONS WILL YOU DELIVER?

UNDERSTAND LUCK, AND MAKE IT WORK FOR YOU.

GOOD LUCK COMES WHEN PREPAREDNESS AND OPPORTUNITY MEET. KEEP YOUR POSITIVE EXPECTATIONS IN MIND AND YOUR SUBCONSCIOUS WILL WORK FOR YOU, SEEKING OUT "LUCK."

DON'T WAIT TO START SETTING AND REACHING YOUR GOALS.

START NOW.

I'VE RECOUNTED MANY CONCEPTS AND TECHNIQUES THAT CAN HELP YOU ATTAIN A RICHER AND MORE FULFILLING LIFESTYLE FOR YOU AND YOUR LOVED ONES.

ALL YOU HAVE TO DO IS PAY THE PRICE AND YOU CAN ACHIEVE THE SUCCESS OF YOUR DREAMS THROUGH SELLING.

YOU CAN BECOME A CHAMPION OF SELLING, A CHAMPION PARENT OR FRIEND, A CHAMPION WIFE OR HUSBAND.

ABOUT THE AUTHOR

Tom Hopkins wasn't born to wealth and privilege. He was a mediocre student and began his work life in construction carrying steel. At the age of 19, he was married with a child on the way and trying to find a better way to support his young family.

Since he wasn't afraid of meeting new people and was known to be somewhat talkative, someone suggested he try selling. After looking around at the people who were dressed well and driving new cars, he decided on the field of real estate.

At the time, real estate was considered an old man's profession. There weren't many women in the field and certainly no teenagers. It took Tom several tries to pass his licensing exam, but he eventually succeeded.

The next hurdle was to find someone to hire him. Visiting real estate offices around town on his way home from his construction job, Tom quickly learned the negative impact of the first impressions he was making.

Eventually, one office manager took pity on him and gave him a job. Tom was instructed to show up at the next office meeting in a suit—not his construction clothes. There was only one challenge, Tom didn't own a suit. He did, however, have a uniform from a band he had been in during high school.

When he arrived at the office meeting, the manager stopped and stared. So did everyone else in the room. Then he heard the manager say, "If that kid in a band uniform can make it in this business, the rest of you better be getting rich!"

Tom's first six months in real estate were anything but successful. He had sold only one home and averaged $42 a month in income. He was down to his last $150 in savings when a man came into the real estate office promoting a three-day sales training seminar with J. Douglas Edwards. Tom hadn't yet heard of either "sales training" or Mr. Edwards. He decided to invest his last bit of savings in the program.

Not only did the light of understanding dawn on Tom that selling is a learned skill, he was so inspired by Mr. Edwards' training that he became an avid student. He attended seminars, read books on selling and even invested in some vinyl records on self-improvement.

Tom applied everything he learned and by the time he turned 27, he was a millionaire salesperson in real estate. He set records that remained unbroken until this century. His last year as a real estate agent, he sold 365 homes—the equivalent of one each day. Grand total, he closed 1,553 real estate transactions in a period of six years.

Then, Tom faced his next hurdle. As much as he loved meeting people and talking with them one-on-one, speaking from stage brought back bad memories of a failed performance in a 1st grade play. However, when he received the many awards he earned and loved, he was often asked to give speeches. Not knowing how to write a speech, Tom started talking about what he did to earn the award—how he sold homes. Everyone wanted to know how he did it so they could do it, too.

Tom turned to J. Douglas Edwards, who by this time had become Tom's mentor. Mr. Edwards said, "You must do what you fear most in order to control your fear." Taking that message to heart, Tom soon became a dedicated student of public speaking and teaching. Seeing the light of understanding dawn on the faces of those who heard his message created a burning desire in him to help as many people as possible to learn how to sell professionally and a new career was born.

Tom taught pre-licensing courses in the field of real estate first. He also taught courses on how to get started in the business. Eventually, this evolved into his current sales training career where he is recognized as America's #1 Sales Trainer and The Builder of Sales Champions.

Tom Hopkins understands both sides of the selling equation. He understands the fears of both buyers and salespeople. Buyers don't want to be "sold" anything. Salespeople fear failure. The selling skills and strategies that Tom Hopkins teaches today reflect an understanding of how to communicate with buyers so they feel confident in making good decisions about the products and services they own. They also are taught in such a manner as to be entertaining and memorable by the sales professionals who seek them out.

ABOUT THE ARTIST

Bob Byrne is an Irish born writer and artist currently living in Spain. Bob has 15 years experience covering product design, caricatures, cartooning, comics and children's books and his comics have appeared in dozens of publications worldwide. He was one of the first publishers of Irish comics and helped kick off the Irish comics industry with MBLEH and The Shiznit. After a few years of self publishing comics in Ireland he took a break to work on his first Graphic Novel, Mister Amperduke, an epic story told without words.

Look for these other titles from SmarterComics and Writers of the Round Table Press:

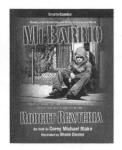

Mi Barrio from SmarterComics
by Robert Renteria as told to Corey Michael Blake
Illustrated by Shane Clester
"Don't let where you came from dictate who you are, but let it be part of who you become." These are the words of successful Latino entrepreneur Robert Renteria who began life as an infant sleeping in a dresser drawer. This poignant and often hard-hitting comic memoir traces Robert's life from a childhood of poverty and abuse in one of the poorest areas of East Los Angeles, to his proud emergence as a business owner and civic leader today.

Shut Up, Stop Whining and Get a Life from SmarterComics
by Larry Winget Illustrated by Shane Clester
Internationally renowned success philosopher, business speaker, and humorist, Larry Winget offers advice that flies in the face of conventional self-help. He believes that the motivational speakers and self-help gurus seem to have forgotten that the operative word in self-help is "self." That is what makes this comic so different. Shut Up, Stop Whining, and Get a Life from SmarterComics forces all responsibility for every aspect of your life right where it belongs— on you. For that reason, this book will make you uncomfortable. Winget won't let you escape to the excuses that we all find so comforting. The only place you are allowed to go to place the blame for everything that has ever happened to you is to the mirror. The last place most of us want to go.

The Art of War from SmarterComics
by Sun Tzu Illustrated by Shane Clester
As true today as when it was written, THE ART OF WAR is a 2,500-year-old classic that is required reading in modern business schools. Penned by the ancient Chinese philosopher and military general Sun Tzu, it reveals how to succeed in any conflict. Read this comic version, and cut to the heart of the message!

Overachievement from SmarterComics
by John Eliot, PH.D. Illustrated by Nathan Lueth

In OVERACHIEVEMENT, Dr. Eliot offers the rest of us the counterintuitive and unconventional concepts that have been embraced by the Olympic athletes, business moguls, top surgeons, salesmen, financial experts, and rock stars who have turned to him for performance enhancement advice. To really ratchet up your performance, you'll need to change the way you think about becoming exceptional-and that means truly being an exception, abnormal by the standards of most, and loving it. Eliot will teach you that overachieving means thriving under pressure-welcoming it, enjoying it, and making it work to your advantage.

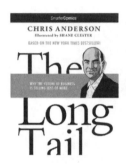

The Long Tail from SmarterComics
by Chris Anderson Illustrated by Shane Clester

The New York Times bestseller that introduced the business world to a future that's already here. Winner of the Gerald Loeb Award for Best Business Book of the Year. In the most important business book since The Tipping Point, Chris Anderson shows how the future of commerce and culture isn't in hits, the high-volume head of a traditional demand curve, but in what used to be regarded as misses--the endlessly long tail of that same curve.

Think and Grow Rich from SmarterComics
by Napoleon Hill Illustrated by Bob Byrne

Think and Grow Rich has sold over 30 million copies and is regarded as the greatest wealth-building guide of all time. Read this comic version and cut to the heart of the message! Written at the advice of millionaire Andrew Carnegie, the book summarizes ideas from over 500 rich and successful people on how to achieve your dreams and get rich doing it. You'll learn money-making secrets - not only what to do but how - laid out in simple steps.

For more information, please visit www.smartercomics.com

The book that inspired the comic...

Available everywhere books are sold.

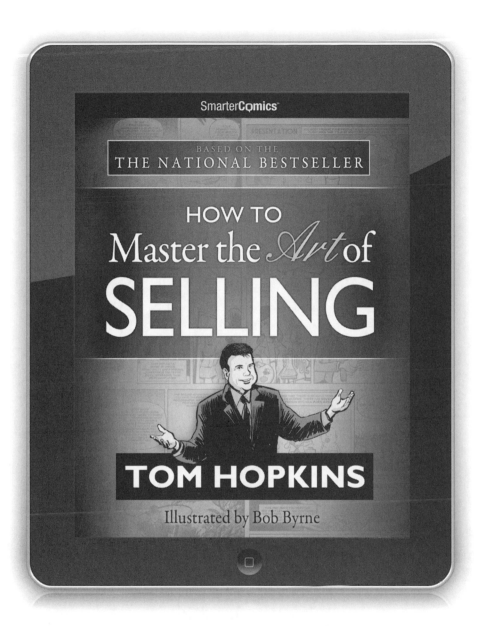

How to Master the Art of Selling and other SmarterComics™ books
are available for download on the iPad and other devices.

www.smartercomics.com

Smarter**Comics**™

Learn
How to Close
More Sales
with
Tom Hopkins

Web: www.tomhopkins.com
Watch sales training videos.
Download MP3s.
See when Tom is coming to your area.
Learn about his amazing 3-day sales boot camp.
Invest in yourself—books, CDs, DVDs and more!

Blog: www.tomhopkins.com/blog
Subscribe and receive free training.

E-mail: helpdesk@tomhopkins.com
Our staff will direct you to the right training for you!

Phone: 480.949.0786
Toll Free (U.S. & Canada) 800.528.0446
(Monday—Friday, 8AM to 5PM, Mountain Standard Time)

SmarterComics™

www.smartercomics.com